PENGUIN MODERN POETS 2

SALVADOR BORGES

Penguin Modern Poets

2

KINGSLEY AMIS

DOM MORAES

PETER PORTER

Penguin Books

Penguin Books Ltd, Harmondsworth, Middlesex, England
Penguin Books Australia Ltd, Ringwood, Victoria, Australia

—

This selection first published 1962
Reprinted 1963, 1965, 1968, 1970

—

Copyright © Penguin Books Ltd, 1962

—

Made and printed in Great Britain
by C. Nicholls & Company Ltd
Set in Monotype Garamond

Contents

ACKNOWLEDGEMENTS

The poems in this selection are taken from the following books, to whose publishers acknowledgement is made: *A Case of Samples* (1956), by Kingsley Amis, published by Victor Gollancz; *A Beginning* (1957, originally published by Parton Press), and *Poems* (1960), by Dom Moraes, published by Eyre & Spottiswoode; *Once Bitten Twice Bitten* (1961), by Peter Porter, published by Scorpion Press.

KINGSLEY AMIS

They Only Move

They only move who travel far,
So whisk me off down roads unsigned
And take me where the good times are.

Whizz past the dance-hall and the bar;
All muffled contact must be blind.
They only move who travel far.

Bortsch, pâté, filthy caviare,
Say I've respectfully declined,
And take me where the good times are.

The social round – Martell, cigar,
Talk about talk – is social grind;
They only move who travel far.

Install me dozing in the car,
Wined, dined, but still unconcubined,
And take me where the good times are.

Lush pastures of the cinema
Will be demanded, once defined,
They only move who travel far.

Fear-indigestion, guilt-catarrh –
If these exist, leave them behind
And take me where the good times are.

Tell me, will movement make or mar?
Then root my body, tell my mind
They only move, who travel far
And take me where the good times are.

The Voice of Authority:
A Language Game

Do this. Don't move. O'Grady says do this,
You get a move on, see, do what I say.
Look lively when I say O'Grady says.

Say this. Shut up. O'Grady says say this,
You talk fast without thinking what to say.
What goes is what I say O'Grady says.

Or rather let me put the point like this:
O'Grady says what goes is what I say
O'Grady says; that's what O'Grady says.

By substituting you can shorten this,
Since any god you like will do to say
The things you like, that's what O'Grady says.

The harm lies not in that, but in that this
Progression's first and last terms are I say
O'Grady says, not just O'Grady says.

Yet it's O'Grady must be out of this
Before what we say goes, not what we say
O'Grady says. Or so O'Grady says.

Creeper

Shaving this morning, I look out of the window
In expectation: will another small
Tendril of ivy, dry and straw-yellow,
Have put its thin clasp on the garden wall?

Oh dear no. A few arid strands, a few
Curled-up leaves, are all that's left of it.
The children pulled it up for something to do,
My mouth sets in its usual post-box slit.

Fled is that vision of a bottle-green
Fur-coat of foliage muffling the pale brick,
Stamping into the flat suburban scene
A proof of beauty, lovable exotic.

Of course, I know ivy will sweetly plump
Itself all over, shyly barge into crannies,
Pull down lump after elegiac lump,
Then tastefully screen ruin from our eyes.

Then it would all become a legal quibble:
Whose what has wrecked what how and by whose
    what;
And moral: is turning stout wall to rubble
A fool's trick in fact, but not in thought?

We should be thankful to be spared all that
When bank-clerk longings get a short answer,
When someone snatches off our silly hat
And drop-kicks it under a steamroller.

Dirty Story

Twice daily, at noon and dusk, if we are lucky,
We hear fresh news of you, an oral cutting
From your unlimited biography.

Today a butcher, you cuckolded the grocer,
Fouling his sugar, in thirty seconds only,
All the while tickling a pretty customer;

Yesterday you posed as a winking parson
Or a gull from the north, cloaking your belly-laughter
With a false voice that mourned for what you'd done;

Tomorrow, in what shrines gaily excreting,
Will you, our champion even if defeated,
Bring down a solemn edifice with one swing?

Hero of single action, epic expert,
Beggar prince and bandit chief of the sexy,
Spry Juan, lifter of the lifted skirt,

What is the secret of your howling successes –
Your tongue never tardy with the punch sentence,
Your you-know-what in fabulous readiness?

Is it no more than the researcher's patience
To ransack life's laboratory, and labour
Ten years distilling salts to be used once;

To nose out the precisely suitable landscape,
The curiously jealous, the uniquely randy,
Then blow them all up in a retort or rape?

If so, your exploits should be read in silence,
Words bred of such travail move none to smiling,
But all to an uneasy reverence:

Reverence at such will to live in stories;
Uneasy, because we see behind your glories
Our own nasty defeats, nastier victories.

On Staying Still

Half-way down the beach
A broken boat lies;
Black in every light,
But squeezed by sand that glows
From black to chocolate
Then ginger-dust. The seas
Soak it for no reason
Each tide-rise, finding it
Dried by the sun for no
Reason, or already wet
With rain before they are near
To strike poses of passion:
Bravery of blind colour,
Noble gesture of spray,
And eloquence of loud noise
That shake not a single spar.
The hulk's only use
Is as mark for pebble-thrower
Or shade for small anemone,
But that is not nothing;
And staying still is more,
When all else is moving
To no end, whether
Or not choice is free.
Good that decay recalls
(By being slow and steady)
Blossom, fruitful change
Of tree to coal, not any
Changeless tidal fury.

Ode to the East-North-East-by-East Wind

You rush to greet me at the corner like
  A cheery chap I can't avoid,
And blow my hair into one leaning spike
  To show you're never unemployed.
You sweating, empty-handed labourer,
You bloody-rowelled, mailless courier,
    Before you rush off somewhere new,
        Just tell us what you do.

We know, of course, you blow the windmills round,
  And that's a splendid thing to do;
Sometimes you pump up water from the ground;
  Why, darling, that's just fine of you!
And round Mount Everest – such fun! – you blow
Gigantic bits of rock about, for no
    Reason – but every little boy
        Must have his little toy.

The old map-makers must have known you well
  (Punch-drunk sea-captains put them wise)
To draw you with an infant's cheeks that swell
  So that they shut your puffy eyes;
No need for you to care or notice where
You kick and writhe and scream in wincing air,
    Telling the void of your distress,
        Raving at emptiness.

Well now, since blowing things apart's your scheme,
  The crying child your metaphor,
Poetic egotists make you their theme,
  Finding in you their hatred for

A world that will not mirror their desire.
Silly yourself, you flatter and inspire
    Some of the silliest of us.
        And is that worth the fuss?

A Note on Wyatt

See her come bearing down, a tidy craft!
Gaily her topsails bulge, her sidelights burn!
There's jigging in her rigging fore and aft,
And beauty's self, not name, limned on her stern.

See at her head the Jolly Roger flutters!
'God, is she fully manned? If she's one short . . .'
Cadet, bargee, longshoreman, shellback mutters;
Drowned is reason that should me comfort.

But habit, like a cork, rides the dark flood,
And, like a cork, keeps her in walls of glass;
Faint legacies of brine tingle my blood,
The tide-wind's fading echoes, as I pass.

Now, jolly ship, sign on a jolly crew:
God bless you, dear, and all who sail in you.

Fair Shares for All

A nude steak posing behind gauze
Wins only gastropaths' applause.

An appetite that can be teased
Must be an appetite diseased.

This diagnosis may have point
When love's delivered with the joint.

A Song of Experience

A quiet start: the tavern, our small party,
    A dark-eyed traveller drinking on his own;
We asked him over when the talk turned hearty,
    And let him tell of women he had known.

He tried all colours, white and black and coffee;
    Though quite a few were chary, more were bold;
Some took it like the host, some like a toffee;
    The two or three who wept were soon consoled.

For seven long years his fancies were tormented
    By one he often wheedled, but in vain;
At last, oh Christ in heaven, she consented,
    And the next day he journeyed on again.

The inaccessible he laid a hand on,
    The heated he refreshed, the cold he warmed.
What Blake presaged, what Lawrence took a stand on,
    What Yeats locked up in fable, he performed.

And so he knew, where we can only fumble,
    Wildly in daydreams, vulgarly in art;
Miles past the point where all delusions crumble
    He found the female and the human heart.

Then love was velvet on a hand of iron
    That wrenched the panting lover from his aim;
Lion rose up as lamb and lamb as lion,
    Nausicaa and Circe were the same.

What counter-images, what cold abstraction
    Could start to quench that living element,
The flash of prophecy, the glare of action?
    – He drained his liquor, paid his score and went.

I saw him, brisk in May, in Juliet's weather,
   Hitch up the trousers of his long-tailed suit,
Polish his windscreen with a chamois-leather,
   And stow his case of samples in the boot.

To Eros

If only we could throw you away,
Garotte you, weight you, sink you in the bay,
  We could start living, we say.

Our girls would all relapse
Back into girls – not all that bright, perhaps,
  But ever such decent chaps,

And when we took them out
To the Sea View, 'Doris', we'd hear them shout,
  'Six pints, please, and a milk stout.'

Should we have the sense to go on
Our labour chief, our thick-lipped roarer gone?
  Or should we re-enter upon

That boring welter of blue,
And at last clear off, not to get shot of you,
  As heroes used to do,

But parching, fed at the oars,
To nab some hodge with bum and scruff like yours
  And bundle him to these shores?

A Bookshop Idyll

Between the GARDENING and the COOKERY
  Comes the brief POETRY shelf;
By the Nonesuch Donne, a thin anthology
  Offers itself.

Critical, and with nothing else to do,
  I scan the Contents page,
Relieved to find the names are mostly new;
  No one my age.

Like all strangers, they divide by sex:
  Landscape near Parma
Interests a man, so does *The Double Vortex*,
  So does *Rilke and Buddha*.

'I travel, you see', 'I think' and 'I can read'
  These titles seem to say;
But *I Remember You, Love is my Creed,
  Poem for J.,*

The ladies' choice, discountenance my patter
  For several seconds;
From somewhere in this (as in any) matter
  A moral beckons.

Should poets bicycle-pump the human heart
  Or squash it flat?
Man's love is of man's life a thing apart;
  Girls aren't like that.

We men have got love well weighed up; our stuff
  Can get by without it.
Women don't seem to think that's good enough;
  They write about it,

And the awful way their poems lay them open
   Just doesn't strike them.
Women are really much nicer than men:
   No wonder we like them.

Deciding this, we can forget those times
   We sat up half the night
Chockfull of love, crammed with bright thoughts,
    names, rhymes,
   And couldn't write.

Act of Kindness

To really give the really valuable,
Or offer the last cigarette,
When shops are shut, to the ungrateful,
Or praise our betters – wishing, we forget

That anything we own is nearly cash,
And to have less of it is dead loss,
That unshared cigarettes are smoke and ash,
That praise is gross.

Not giving should be not living; how to live,
How to deal with any wish to give
When the gift gets stuck to the fingers?
We give nothing we have,
So smiling at strangers

Best suits our book – they cannot tell
Our own from others' words; generous
With common property we seem amiable;
Not to draw a knife
Looks like an act of kindness,
And is, acted to the life.

Lessons

How long, when hand of master is withdrawn,
Will hand of pupil move as if it stayed?
The books once closed, the classroom blind run down,
Who thinks of lessons now there is no need?

Docility, of feature or of mind,
Is glad to wither when the tongue is free;
Even if one phrase, one shared thought, remained,
Ten more will come and go by half past four.

Therefore let all who teach discard this pride,
That anything is learnt except to please;
When fingers touch, or how love's names are said,
Like any lessons, change with time and place;

So here and now, with individual care,
This one sole way hand may be laid on hand,
Voice only with one voice may learn to cry,
And thus tongue lie with tongue, thus mind with
        mind.

But out of school, all ways the hand will move,
Forget the private hour, and touch the world;
The voice will bawl, slur the accent of love,
The tongue slop sweets, the mind lounge home
        expelled.

Bed and Breakfast

Sometimes a parting leaves only a room
That frames a void in yellow wallpapers,
Unpersoned by such brief indifferent use;
But love, once broken off, builds a response
In the final turning pause that sees nothing
Is left, and grieves though nothing happened here.

So, stranger, when you come here to unpack,
To look like me excited on the garden,
Expect from me nothing but a false wish
That, going, you ignore all other partings,
And find no ghosts that growl or whinny of
Kisses from nowhere, negligible tears.

Masters

That horse whose rider fears to jump will fall,
Riflemen miss if orders sound unsure;
They only are secure who seem secure;
    Who lose their voice, lose all.

Those whom heredity or guns have made
Masters, must show it by a common speech;
Expected words in the same tone from each
    Will always be obeyed.

Likewise with stance, with gestures, and with face;
No more than mouth need move when words are said,
No more than hand to strike, or point ahead;
    Like slaves, limbs learn their place.

In triumph as in mutiny unmoved,
These make their public act their private good,
Their words in lounge or courtroom understood,
    But themselves never loved.

The eyes that will not look, the twitching cheek,
The hands that sketch what mouth would fear to own,
Only these make us known, and we are known
    Only as we are weak:

By yielding mastery the will is freed,
For it is by surrender that we live,
And we are taken if we wish to give,
    Are needed if we need.

Departure

For one month afterwards the eye stays true,
And sees the other's face held still and free
Of ornament; then tires of peering down
A narrow vista, and the month runs out.

Too young, this eye will claim the merit of
A faithful sentry frozen at his post
And not a movement seen; yet ranges over
Far other tracts, its object lost, corrupt.

Nor should I now swell to halloo the names
Of feelings that no one needs to remember,
Nor caper with my posy of wilted avowals
To clutter up your path I should wish clear.

Perhaps it is not too late to crane the eye
And find you, distant and small, but as you are;
If not, I will retain you honestly blurred,
Not a bland refraction of sweet mirrors.

Here is Where

Here, where the ragged water
Is twilled and spun over
Pebbles backed like beetles,
Bright as beer-bottles
Bits of it like snow beaten,
Or milk boiling in saucepan . . .

Going well so far, eh?
But soon, I'm sorry to say,
The here-where recipe
Will have to intrude its I,
Its main verb want,
Its this at some tangent.

What has this subject
Got to do with that object?
Why drag in
All that water and stone?
Scream the place down here,
There's nobody there.

The country, to townies,
Is hardly more than nice,
A window-box, pretty
When the afternoon's empty;
When a visitor waits,
The window shuts.

The End

The mirror holds: small common objects fill
Its eye impatient, sore with keeping still.
   The book, the person stupefy,
   Merely because they fill its eye.

The mirror breaks, and fragments wheel and flare
– Before their mercury dissolves in air –
   To seize the person for one look,
   To catch one image of the book.

Nocturne

Under the winter street-lamps, near the bus-stop,
Two people with nowhere to go fondle each other,
Writhe slowly in the entrance to a shop.
In the intervals of watching them, a sailor
Yaws about with an empty beer-flagon,
Looking for something good to smash it on.

Mere animals: on this the Watch Committee
And myself seem likely to agree;
But all this fumbling about, this wasteful
Voiding of sweat and breath – is that *animal*!

Nothing so sure and economical.

These keep the image of another creature
In crippled versions, cocky, drab and stewed?
What beast holds off its paw to gesture,
Or gropes towards being understood?

Wrong Words

Half-shut, our eye dawdles down the page
Seeing the word love, the word death, the word life,
Rhyme-words of poets in a silver age:
Silver of the bauble, not of the knife.

Too fluent, drenching with confectionery
One image, one event's hard outline,
The words of failure's voluptuary
Descant around love – love of a routine.

There follow high words from a thwarted child
Rightly denied what it would foul, threatening
Grown-ups with its death, eager to gild
The pose of writhing with the pose of resigning.

But loneliness, the word never said,
Pleads to be recognized through their conceits;
Behind their frantic distortion lies the dread,
Unforced, unblurred, of real defeats:

Their real ladies would not follow the book,
Wrong ladies, happy with wrong words, wrong lives;
Careening now, they blazed, while none would look,
The distress signals of their superlatives.

Against Romanticism

A traveller who walks a temperate zone
Woods devoid of beasts, roads that please the foot –
   Finds that its decent surface grows too thin:
   Something unperceived fumbles at his nerves.
To please an ingrown taste for anarchy
   Torrid images circle in the wood,
And sweat for recognition up the road,
   Cramming close the air with their bookish cries.
All senses then are glad to gasp: the eye
   Smeared with garish paints, tickled up with ghosts
That brandish warnings or an abstract noun;
   Melodies from shards, memories from coal,
Or saws from powdered tombstones thump the ear;
   Bodies rich with heat wriggle to the touch,
And verbal scents made real spellbind the nose;
   Incense, frankincense; legendary the taste
Of drinks or fruits or tongues laid on the tongue.
   Over all, a grand meaning fills the scene,
And sets the brain raging with prophecy,
   Raging to discard real time and place,
Raging to build a better time and place
   Than the ones which give prophecy its field
To work, the calm material for its rage,
   And the context which makes its prophecy.

Better, of course, if images were plain,
   Warnings clearly said, shapes put down quite still
Within the fingers' reach, or else nowhere;
   But complexities crowd the simplest thing,
And flaw the surface that they cannot break.
   Let us make at least visions that we need:
Let mine be pallid, so that it cannot
   Force a single glance, form a single word;

An afternoon long-drawn and silent, with
   Buildings free from all grime of history,
The people total strangers, the grass cut,
   Not long, voluble swooning wilderness.
And green, not parched or soured by frantic suns
   Doubling the commands of a rout of gods,
Nor trampled by the havering unicorn ;
   Let the sky be clean of officious birds
Punctiliously flying on the left;
   Let there be a path leading out of sight,
And at its other end a temperate zone:
   Woods devoid of beasts, roads that please the foot.

The Last War

The first country to die was normal in the evening,
Ate a good but plain dinner, chatted with some friends
Over a glass, and went to bed soon after ten;
And in the morning was found disfigured and dead.
  That was a lucky one.

At breakfast the others heard about it, and kept
Their eyes on their plates. Who was guilty? No one knew,
But by lunch-time three more would never eat again.
The rest appealed for frankness, quietly cocked their
    guns,
  Declared 'This can't go on.'

They were right. Only the strongest turned up for tea:
The old ones with the big estates hadn't survived
The slobbering blindfold violence of the afternoon.
One killer or many? Was it a gang, or all-against-all?
  Somebody must have known.

But each of them sat there watching the others, until
Night came and found them anxious to get it over.
Then the lights went out. A few might have lived, even
    then;
Innocent, they thought (at first) it still mattered what
  You had or hadn't done.

They were wrong. One had been lenient with his
    servants;
Another ran an island brothel, but rarely left it;
The third owned a museum, the fourth a remarkable gun;
The name of a fifth was quite unknown, but in the end
  What was the difference? None.

Homicide, pacifist, crusader, cynic, gentile, jew
Staggered about moaning, shooting into the dark.
Next day, to tidy up as usual, the sun came in
When they and their ammunition were all used up,
   And found himself alone.

Upset, he looked them over, to separate, if he could,
The assassins from the victims, but every face
Had taken on the flat anonymity of pain;
And soon they'll all smell alike, he thought, and felt sick,
   And went to bed at noon.

The Sources of the Past

A broken flower-stem, a broken vase,
    A matchbox torn in two and thrown
Among the scraps of glass:
    At a last meeting, these alone
Record its ruptures, bound its violence,
    And make a specious promise to retain
This charted look of permanence
    In the first moment's pain.

But now the door slams, the steps retreat;
    Into one softness night will blur
The diverse, the hard street;
    And memory will soon prefer
That polished set of symbols, glass and rose
    (By slight revision), to the real mess
Of stumbling, arguing, yells, blows:
    To real distress.

All fragments of the past, near and far,
    Come down to us framed in a calm
No contemplations jar;
    But they grub it up from lapse of time,
And, could we strip that bland order away,
    What vulgar agitation would be shown:
What aimless hauntings behind clay,
    What fussing behind stone?

The Triumph of Time

When Party-Member Lech lifts up his knout,
We know that's funny and unfunny;
When he gives you a clout,

That's funny, your friends agree,
But for you the joke falls flat.
(Now love's different, do you see.)

We can, we must, we will put up with that:
A man can't go on laughing all the time,
Or minding being laughed at,

And, far from being mere slime or grime,
This is the origin, I propound,
Of our ideas concerning the sublime.

That's fair; but will it still be, when we're found
Fustily grinning at a leg-show,
Funny and unfunny the other way round?

The Value of Suffering

Surrounded for years with all the most assured
Tokens of size and sense – the broad thick table
Triple-banked with food, too much to eat, and
    flowers
Too mixed and many to smell, and ladies too
Ready, sating ambition before it formed –
He went on hunting in the right costume,
Postured among the stolid falconers
(But lobbed his purses to the lutanists),
And, as the eldest son, was first in all
Exercises of eye, mouth, hand and loins.

Then mildew broke across the azure hangings,
Mould on his leather; his horse declined to stir
For all he made it bleed, and his men had time
To jeer at him before the fire took them.
Now, shaven head abased, sandalled feet slow,
He roams the crumbled courts and speaks to none;
But all crave blessing from his hand that clasps
A book, who never feared its pretty sword.

What a shame that a regal house must founder,
Its menials die, its favourites undergo
Unheard-of-rape, to emphasize a contract,
To point one thing out to one person;
Especially since the person could have seen
What it was all about by watching faces
After his father's joke, instead of laughing,
By changing places with his groom,
    By sixty seconds' thought.

DOM MORAES

Cainsmorning

Having eliminated his dear brother
He let tears fall and wandered off alone,
Blaming himself in whispers for another
Error, yet knowing that he could not atone:

'In this day's silence I am unattended,
Yet (understand me) I did all for good:
Though I am sorry now that I have ended
My thirst for freedom in my brother's blood.'

The morning changed, grew chilly and transparent.
Suddenly all the light shrank and was gone:
And then at last his guilt became apparent
Even to him, yet he went slowly on.

The mountains sneered, the river whispered Slayer!
He felt a saraband start in his brain,
And turned his face to heaven, and saw his prayer
Melt in the cold, the grey, the faceless rain.

Autobiography

A child, the soft-pawed sky held up my kites.
Tumultuous images rose from the mud.
My eyes like fish flickered through sunken lights
Under the poems dancing in my blood.
And from this great, this all-gate-breaking flood,
My thoughts like pincers lifted tastes and sights.
My heart delved down to love, knowledge of God,
Waited the king in sandals on the heights.

But even then I was as cold as stone,
Sinking among the ripples of the crowd,
And now all my desire is to atone
For an unfriendly springtime, webbed in cloud.
I remember my grandmother, crescent-browed,
Falling from Time, leaf-light, too much alone:
And my grandfather, who was small and proud.
Tumult of images, where have you gone?

The ageing chemist in his drawing-room, terse,
Gentle: the sea like soapsuds in the night,
Seen from a ship: the moon, leprous, inverse,
Rising: the girl at Hanoi with her white
Hands and dog's eyes, dripping with amber light:
Have these things shaped me for the craft of verse?
Do they remain, giving a sad insight?
And have I changed for better or for worse?

I have grown up, I think, to live alone,
To keep my old illusions, sometimes dream
Glumly that I am unloved and forlorn,
Run away from strangers, often seem

Unreal to myself in the pulpy warmth of a sunbeam.
I have grown up, hand on the primal bone,
Making the poem, taking the word from the stream,
Fighting the sand for speech, fighting the stone.

At Seven O'Clock

The masseur from Ceylon, whose balding head
Gives him a curious look of tenderness,
Uncurls his long crushed hands above my bed
As though he were about to preach or bless.

His poulterer's fingers pluck my queasy skin,
Shuffle along my side, and reach the thigh.
I note however that he keeps his thin
Fastidious nostrils safely turned away.

But sometimes the antarctic eyes glance down,
And the lids drop to hood a scornful flash:
A deep ironic knowledge of the thin
Or gross (but always ugly) human flesh.

Hernia, goitre and the flowering boil
Lie bare beneath his hands, for ever bare.
His fingers touch the skin: they reach the soul.
I know him in the morning for a seer.

Within my mind he is reborn as Christ:
For each blind dawn he kneads my prostrate thighs,
Thumps on my buttocks with his fist
And breathes, Arise.

The Pilgrims

Spiky with pines like wire brushes, clad
In patchwork snow, the mountains rise across
The dry bronze-coloured bloodstain of the plain
Where we once walked, bearing a heavy loss.

But here the rocks explode into fresh water
Around us, and green-tasselled palm-trees bend,
Brushed by a wind's feather:
We have found the promised land.

Now our unrest returns; we burn again,
Thinking, as we look back towards the few
Sponge-textured plants festering in the far plain,
That we have nothing to look forward to.

For Dorothy

Where you lived, when the fighting planes came over,
The houses shrank into their bricks, and then
Suddenly fell down, and then the river
Went red and pulpy, and the limbs of men
Tumbled around you where you stood, a child,
Wondering upward at what fell from heaven
To break your toys.

     Years later, when you smiled,
All was explained, though nothing was forgiven.

Catullus

Under your cold eye, colour of the sea,
Rome failed to burn, but many strangers slept
With Lesbia, till you raged, becoming free,
Clapping your hands, mocking when others wept.

Aurelius unlipped his donkey's mouth,
Braying after boys. You spent no sudden breath.
On sodden decks, when you at last went south,
You mourned illusion and a brother's death.

You set up house, Catullus, where the flocks
Of lice found pasture in the peasant's locks,
Where corn was suffocated by the clod.

You raged at Rome: Rome giggled, unaware,
Your terrible iambics lashed the air,
Winnowing the wind like the flails of God.

Bells for William Wordsworth

Today they brought me a message: Wordsworth was
    dead.
'My God,' I said. 'My God. I can hardly believe it.'
'Just as you like,' they answered. 'Take it or leave it,
 He has sunk into April as into the depths of a lake,
 Leaving his eyes ajar in the house of his head.'
'Are you sure,' I said, 'that you haven't made a mistake?'

'Oh no,' they said, 'not a hope. We knew him too well,
 A gloomy considering bloke with the nose of a preacher:
 A poet in fact, with a charming affection for Nature:
 Milkmaids (you know) and the shadows of clouds on the
    land.
 His work is carefully studied in colleges still.
 We shall not forget nor forgo it, while colleges stand.'

And I said, 'I grant you that Wordsworth lies chilly in
    Grasmere
And his bones are absolved and dissolved in the tears of
    the rain.
I grant he is one with the plant and the fossil again,
His flesh has gone back into soil and his eyes into stones
And the roots and shoots of a new life push each year
Through the sad rotten fragments of his bones.

'But although each Spring brings a newer death to those
    bones,
 I have seen him risen again with the crocus in Spring.
 I have turned my ear to the wind, I have heard him
    speaking.
 I shrank from the bony sorrow in his face.
 Yet still I hear those pedagogic tones
 Droning away the snow, our old disgrace.'

The Island

I

THE BURNING

Like the birdflights migrating from the island
We flutter round and click our tongues above
The unwieldy hero pyred upon the sand

And a girl murmurs guiltily as a dove
Over the massive skull, bronze scales for eyes,
That looks upon her and ignores her love.

The sun he loved has put a wreath of flies
Around his mouth, so to renew his song
– Humming that tells us of the paradise

Where he is citizen, where long
Dew-softened grass bandages his torn feet;
Where the dragon comes to him and does no wrong.

The shore softens; the day has left its heat.
Vaguely we lift our hands, touching the pyre.
We cannot live where he lives, dumb, complete,

In a green fastness come to his desire.
We know the dragon of the island still
Treads in the mountains, coughing up its fire.

We live with that, the obsolete and evil.

II
THE COMING

We knew him by the hollow eyes and beard
And asked was he a prophet: when he said
No, we pretended that we hadn't heard.

With spider-coloured flowers we dressed his head,
Bowed clumsily to him, and then requested
That he be helpful and restore our dead

Hero to us, before the dragon wasted
The entire land. We bribed him with strong beer.
He soon agreed to do as we suggested.

We came to where the hero slept, austere
In the crude fires of noon. The women wept,
Swaying their long hair like trees. A kind of fear

Came to us all. We watched. The prophet stepped
Closer, and blinked into the sleeping eyes.
He laid his hands on. Still the hero slept.

We do not blame the prophet: he is wise
And after all a stranger, coming from
Lands where the dead, when hands are laid on, rise.

It is not like that in our island home.

III
THE CONQUEST

The mainland dwellers wished to colonize.
At first beaked ships came sniffing round our coasts.
Later their generals, following that advice,

Unrolled upon our shores the sea-voiced hosts.
There was no clash of arms: we simply fled,
Quitting the sunlight, dehydrated ghosts,

Gauze men, unbarbered, ragged and unled,
Fingering weapons we could not employ,
Wishing our hero were not quite so dead –

And then we said: The dragon will destroy
Them, since he put our hero to eclipse.
And this thought brought us mirth and simple joy.

Hiding in caves all day, where water drips
Always through fissures, we felt no more shame,
But an expectant pleasure. From their ships

Their hero stalked, while they cried out his name,
Iron on his chest, and on his lips a joke
We smiled with faith.

    But when the moment came
He slew the dragon with a single stroke.

IV

AFTERWARDS

It was not war but mutual defeat.
Our conquerors shrivelled in the island sun.
Lighter than leaves, they drifted to our feet,

Dying of peace, and not as some have done,
Fighting. Their weapons hung about their walls
When they resigned the portion they had won.

We, also dying, sit quietly in our halls,
Feed off our nails, watch the birds flying and creep
Early to bed: for there the hero calls.

We are visited by angels in our sleep.
They have faces like dogs, with lustrous eyes.
Their noses twitch as though they longed to weep.

It is their sad and permanent disguise.
We tremble at their touch, an icy fever.
Yet still we follow them, for they are wise,

Through the naves of forest, to the river
That whispers to the shores on which we stand
Silent, and human there, forever

Taking the truthful water in our hand.

The Final Word

Since I was ten I have not been unkind
To anyone save those who were most close:
Of my close friends one of the best is blind,
One deaf, and one a priest who can't write prose.
None has a quiet mind.

Deep into night my friends with tired faces
Break language up for one word to remain,
The tall forgiving word nothing effaces,
Though without maps it travel, and explain
A pure truth in all places.

Yet death, if it should fall on us, would be
Only the smallest settling into beds:
Our last words lost because Eternity
Made its loud noise above our lifted heads
Before we ceased to see.

But, all made blind and deaf, the final word
Bequeathed by us, at the far side of
Experience, waits: there neither man nor bird
Settles, except with knowledge, or much love.
There Adam's voice is heard.

And my true love, a skylark in each eye,
Walks the small grass, and the small frightened things
Scurry to her for comfort, and can't die
While she still lives, and all the broken Kings
Kneel to her and know why.

Because she turns, her love at last expressed,
Into my arms: and then I cannot die.
I have furnished my heart to be her nest
For even if at dusk she choose to fly
Afterwards she must rest.

Song

I sowed my wild oats
Before I was twenty.
Drunkards and turncoats
I knew in plenty.
Most friends betrayed me.
Each new affair
Further delayed me.
I didn't care.

I put no end to
The life that led me
The friends to lend to,
The bards who bled me.
Every bad penny
Finds its own robber.
My beds were many
And my cheques rubber.

Then, with the weather worse,
To the cold river,
I came reciting verse
With a hangover.
You shook a clammy hand.
How could I tell you
Then that wild oats died and
Brighter grain grew?

Now, once more wintertime,
We sit together.
In your bright forelock Time
Gives me fair weather.

Soon will a summer break
Well worth the having.
Then shall our hearts awake
Into our loving.

Snow on a Mountain

That dream, her eyes like rocks studded the high
Mountain of her body that I was to climb.
  One moment past my hands had swum
  The chanting streams of her thighs:
Then I was lost, breathless among the pines.

Alone, alone with the nervous noise of water,
Climbing, I hoped to emerge on a path, but I knew
  When the spurred trees were past
  I should go on no farther
But fall there, dazzled by the miles of snow.

My dream was broken by the knock of day.
Yet, within my mind, these pictures linger:
  I touch her with my clumsy words of love
  And sense snow in her eye,
Mists, and the winds that warn, Stranger, O stranger!

Being Married

When I awake (he said) I shall be lonely,
O feel my loneliest ever by your side;
For I have dropped my root, and stuck: you only
Move through a night of sleep, conscious of right.
  Beloved conquering bride,
My kisses lanced your veins with veins of light.

O take my angel in your sleeping flesh.
I killed him from me, wrestling with your belly,
Wrenched to the contact and the bitter flash
Which you stir well, better than verse perhaps.
  Lost angel, now how easily
The ritual nights will come, and roots collapse.

I lost in night must hear you breathe in whispers,
Your hater now for spendthrift of my breath:
Lost in the night we fought; we rushed together
At frontiers of our miles of loneliness
  And lived, and parted at a gate
Where the last touch of lips was meant to bless.

The Garden

I wake and find myself in love:
And this one time I do not doubt.
I only fear, and wander out
To hold long parley with a dove.

The innocent and the guilty, met
Here in the garden, feel no fear.
But I'm afraid of you, my dear.
There was a reason: I forget.

And I by shyness am undone
And can't go out for fear I meet
My poems dancing down the street
Telling your name to everyone.

The lichen peels along the wall.
My conversation bores the dove.
He knows it all: that I'm in love
And you care much and not at all.

I shall stay here and keep my word.
Glumly I wait to marry dust.
It grieves me only that I must
Speak not to you, but to a bird.

Afternoon Tea

She poured the tea. Vaguely I watched her hands.
The mask was fitted: in my wandering dream
Were boulder-broken valleys, a strange land.
Remote, astonished, I stood by a stream
Holding her hand in mine. The afternoon
Moved in my bones. Sun flecked the leaves and sand.
And she seemed fragile: but with roots in stone,
Blue-veined, the flower of a northern land.

And then things changed: and do not ask me why:
But privately and gently, as her hand
Might let mine fall, all love became a lie:
My gesture broke upon a dream beyond
Scones and my witty mouth and those chic cups
And the strange look that fussed me into rhyme:
An inarticulate wincing at the lips:
At last the key: and I came back to Time.

There to achieve a root, slowly to grow,
Is all my will. Here no one can elude
Desire, but in this city, when I go,
I'll leave a bedtime and destructive mood.
Her anger dwells there, wistful; and my drouth
Burns in the shadow country of a dream
Where her cool mouth flows backward from my mouth
And her long hands sustain a golden stream.

Card Game

Unfold the table: cut and deal the cards.
It would be perfect, if you only lacked
That strange hypocrisy: but deal the cards.
These pictured kings and royalties contract
The great dishevelled world of my distress
Into an unsuspected tenderness.

What story did you tell behind my back?
I know it: from my worst you made your best.
You are the knave, the liar in the pack,
Too human always, childheart, to be honest.
Yet something we have shared compels your claim
To an emotion that I cannot name.

You are as brutal as a child, yet shy
And like a child: my memories turn to ink:
Buried in all our pasts are greed and lies,
Anger and hateful actions: and I think
That frigid chumminess of my boyhood
Came closest to a deep material good.

O now we stare, sight with lost stances blended,
Each to himself a shadow on a screen.
Tomorrow our accustomed life is ended.
Plans must be made, this dull familiar scene
Be done with, roots torn up where we began.
Smiling at you, I know we shall not smile together again.

One of Us

We used to drink in the same place.
I never spoke to him, because
Of knowing him only by the face:
A strange face: something in it was
Naked, shrinking, like a snail
Curled inside its tissue town,
That does not know what winds prevail
Until its own leaf is brought down.
Leaf-shaped the room in which for years
The poets and their friends would drink
Where most transmuted drink to tears
And some transmitted tears to ink.
And there behind the folded door
He huddled, nibbling his desire.
A glass would smash upon the floor
And swaddled in its logs the fire
Hiccupped out uncertain light.
The lonely drinkers would start crying,
Or fled in greatcoats to the night,
But not until the fire was dying
Could he bear to rise, his gaze
Like a priest who says Amen:
And not until the clock said ten
A baffled clinging in the eyes.
Then the thick lips breathed apart.
Stumbling, as if he had not meant
To come at all, he would depart.
I often wondered where he went.
Did he launch out on fruitless flights
Till intercepted by a bus?
This lonely starer at the lights,
Was he another one of us,

Who when the landlord's burly wife,
Asbestos-gloved, clenched out the breath
Of the fire, each night of life,
Took one step nearer into death?

An Ordinary Care

Visit the rumoured stranger on the stair,
Though you to find him must go round and round;
Upon the lowest landing, by a bare
Window that opens on to barer ground,
Plain in plain light, the one you seek is found.

These months of early cold, unripe November,
A slant of light, trembling, a woman's tone,
You so much loved, and wanted to remember
Against its end, or yours. But he, alone,
Keeps inward excellence of skeleton.

Then stand: say nothing: nothing you believe,
Or think you do, will he: but smile: and sigh:
Your hand, your hands in his, like blows relieve
Not helplessness or sorrow, but self-pity.
He missed, one day in Spring, his time to die.

From Tibet

I

For me my dark words are
Quickened by your bright hair,
But I have come too far
To a strange country where
Tree-fingers point towards
Darkness, and I lack words.

The yaks like clumps of wool
Stump through red poison-flowers,
So red, so beautiful,
A dream rises and towers
Beyond me, till I stand,
Your hand warm in my hand.

But I must ride with Das,
A small man quick with hope
Toward the invaded pass
Up the lichen-rusted slope.
Cloud-fastened, ice-ribbed, where
A few hawks shriek and stare.

I shall keep warm above
The valleys hazed and far
For these days I find love
In poem, wind and star.
Wiser than I am wise,
You have lent me your eyes.

II

Today the rare pale sun
Appears, and the mules snort.
Das writes his press report –
We have seen no Chinese.
No fighting has begun.
The hawks sleep in the trees.

I have seen enough
Of this valley and this death.
I would not waste my breath
Mourning, but be a hawk
Who would take wing far off
Before the approaching dark.

Like cinders the red flowers
Brush fire across my sleeve.
I shall remount and leave
Taking no backward look,
And then collect these hours
In a travel book.

My book will tell the truth
But it will not be true,
Till I return to you,
My truth, my miracle.
While I keep my old faith
In you, I shall write well.

My page will be of stone
Where the bright water scrawls
The truth of Time, which falls
From times when, you not there,
I would recall, alone,
The colour of your hair.

Gone Away

My native city rose from sea,
Its littered frontiers wet and dark.
Time came too soon to disembark
And rain like buckshot sprayed my head.
My dreams, I thought, lacked dignity.
So I got drunk and went to bed.

But dreamt of you all night, and felt
More lonely at the break of day
And trod, to brush the dream away,
The misted pavements where rain fell.
There the consumptive beggars knelt,
Voiced with the thin voice of a shell.

The records that those pavements keep,
Bronze relics from the beggar's lung,
Oppress me, fastening my tongue.
Seawhisper in the rocky bay
Derides me, and when I find sleep,
The parakeets shriek that away.

Except in you I have no rest,
For always with you I am safe:
Who now am far, and mime the deaf
Though you call gently as a dove.
Yet each day turns to wander west:
And every journey ends in love.

The Guardians

The guardians said: 'Wait for him if you like.
Often he comes when called, this time he may.
You will know it when the hawk, ruffling to strike,
Glimpses his white coat, and forbears to slay.
If it be in his mind, he will
Come at twilight to the dark pool.'

I said, 'Since childhood I have watched for him,
Burying this head so heavy with so much
Confusion, in my hands, while the world, dim
With many twilights, spun toward his touch.
Through a child's fingers then the time of love
Flowered in his eyes, and became alive.

'Sorrow walks after love: our childhood dies.
My twenty years of fighting came to this:
The brown eyes of my love looked in my eyes,
Beautiful in farewell, at our last kiss.
Her eyes like his eyes dealt so deep a wound,
Until he touch it, it will itch in wind.'

The guardians with stone flesh and faces of
Crumpled and heavy linen, stared at me.
With neither pity nor the fear of love,
Each stony hand clenched on a stony knee.
Grinding like a crushed stone, each voice said, 'Let
Time pass. Pray you are not too late.'

The Visitor

After the sleepy throats of the first birds
Had creaked a madrigal into the sky,
A thin sun rose to separate the curds
Of sea, but my drab visitor stayed by
My bedside, and assailed me with the words
That had flailed sleep from me. Though I still fought,
Attempting flights to day, or back to sleep,
The cobwebs in his eyes, and on his coat
Moored all my life to him, till in the deep
Trenches of his dark language I was caught.

Rain followed sun: and on the wall outside
The flowers shuddered and shed sudden tears.
The room was bare: there was nowhere to hide,
Nowhere to go. He whispered in my ears,
Two shells filled with the memory of the tide:
'You are afraid. Often I've watched you run
Panting up blackened stairs, flight after flight.
On the next landing there was always one
Who made retreat. I bring your darkness light.
Meeting will happen by my changing sun.

'Name whom you seek. In me he will appear.
Call me Nijinsky, and applaud my dance.
A rugger blue, and offer me some beer.
An editor: plague me for an advance.
Or think instead the one you love is here,
Her brown eyes happy, breathless from her bike:
And very gently kiss, as once you kissed,
Or take me for your enemy, and strike
The mask I wear, and I shall not resist.
I shall be God, or anything you like.

'I shall be he whom you will never find,
Except in me: I am the last pretence:
Dark angel of the world, who moves behind
Dayfall, and whispers truth to innocence,
Hurting it into tears: yet I am kind.
Acceptance sleeps in light, abandoning there
The tedious climb, the fighting in the heart.'
He paused and whispered: 'Else you must prepare
To ask what godheads or what kings depart,
And I shall answer, shadows on the stair.'

In Meadows

The swift romantic touch among the meadows
Brought her around from ether of the thyme:
How long had she lain sleeping in the shadows,
Leafwandered, not rebutting, fighting Time?
How long lain in, not with and of the meadows,
A silken figure in a sylvan rhyme?

Whose was that whisper running down the meadows?
O whose that touch at which she felt no shame?
Her body wakened, clad in flesh of meadow:
She had become herself, but not the same.
If still she felt the shadows
They had now another name.

So she turned home, but now the empty winter
And thorny forest fumed upon her breath:
A pulse of love knocked at the door to enter:
The touch lay frosty in her room beneath.
She'll carry always, changed one, at the centre,
An ice of life, to crag amidst her death.

Ophelia

Lice in the pale weeds of her crown
Creep: she is pendulumed in Time:
The heavy sea will wrap her down,
Drenched in its phosphorus and lime.

Her small transparent veins shed blood.
Poor child: those tremulous and grave
Walkers with stilts for legs bring food.
Each wrings his white hands like a wave.

For soon, by this departing light,
The tide, climbing its rocky stair,
Will whisper in her bones all night
And slowly loosen her long hair.

With idiot motion in the sea
Her driftwood shape will travel far.
Never will it seek land, for she
Has fled our tributes and our war.

The shape we trace upon the tide
Departs, with many stars above.
The child who touched us in the side
Sleeps now, forgetful, and with love.

Glitter of Pebbles

The sun was witness when his eyes appeared,
Glitter of pebbles through the crinkled water.
Rising, he stripped away the flesh of river,
    Bared shoulder, arm and flank,
While sand broke use in green and rock in water
As though the desert from his body drank.

Then, from the thorn and stain, the tiny creatures
Lost in their life came quivering to his hands:
Lizards and snakes and squirrels and jerboas,
    Quail from the vultured sky,
Drawn by the essential elements combined
– Air, water, earth – in the timeless boundless body.

Thus in his flesh the world was recreated.
This I saw happen, and it fed my hope –
Happy the land created, uncreated,
    Happy, happy in his stream
I longed to splash, but down the gentle slope
Of sleep rolled, to awake. I should not dream.

Yesterday night's creative ecstasy,
I know, too often makes today's despair,
Yet, hopeful to the end, I turned to see,
    And I saw myself alone
With all around the ache of space, the glare
Of heat, and at my feet the stone, the stone.

That Was

That was an innocent country:
Warlock and dwarf, the hairy forest, dragons
Somewhere there, they said,
Though never seen, sometimes heard:
Somewhere in the hills, the hermit's cavern
Where all was forgiven.

There dying would only be the trek to sleep
Or waking through tall mirrors of a dream:
In spite of which all were afraid to die.
The golden princess had no remedy
When the dragon arrived
But to surrender to his lechery.

Opened her eyes but found herself awake
Or asleep perhaps in the same
Dream by the sleeping unsuffering lake
Where her grief as simple as dying
Pressed her body into the shape of a tear
Lying by embroidered leaves
To fade upon the handkerchiefs of water.

That tyrant was limpid.
With his iron guard of poets and his liars,
He bubbled through stone-walled halls of life
Sucking upon his tide
Like tiny coloured pebbles, chilled desires.

At a river's end
Streams gulp and sweat, expiring in the sand.

PETER PORTER

Forefathers' View of Failure

Men with religion as their best technique,
Who built bush churches six days a week,
Stencilled failure's index on their brains.
Whisky laced the mucous of their heads,
Flushed their pores, narrow-bored their veins,
But they were building still on their death-beds
Having no life but the marking-time of work,
Sleeping collapsed outside despair and talk.

These ancestors might pity or despise
Free-will, willing despair into lives.
They used sin as a weather-telling limb,
Climbed to bed with a bottle, took
Days on a bender but never had a whim
Like protest or millenium from a book –
These narrow fates had a viciousness
They drank for, but no vicariousness.

It would seem failure to them to have
Knowledge a Scottish textbook never gave
Or to fear regular love on an iron bedstead
With children lying awake a wall away.
Their sophistication was only to be dead
After drinking the sun down into the bay.
Their gulps shake out time, their health
Is in country roses, a hard red wealth.

The weatherboard churches bleached white
As the calcimined crosses round them invite,
Like the War Memorial with ten names,
Eyes up to plain Heaven. It is hard to see

Past good intentions – on any visitor the same
Wind trespasses ashore from a wailing sea.
In this new land the transplanted grasses root,
Waving as sulkily as through old falling soot.

Once Bitten, Twice Bitten;
Once Shy, Twice Shy

The trap setter in a steel dawn
Picks up his dead rabbits and goes home
Whistling: his tune lies over the wet fields
In the shrinking morning shadows.
The gift of morning life brings
Five broken backs for the rabbits
Dangling in his hessian wrap.
In his own house an old mother
Wastes herself for a busy cancer,
She has always sacrificed flesh and time
For others – a thin heart hates a fat man
In the same room of waiting,
And outside, two children chase
A cockerel from a hen; their sister,
In love with a school teacher,
Pushes back the sex in her measuring blouse.
Now the house basks in bridal sun
Brimming with doves. This is where
The dead rabbits come, giving life
To the fat dog and his mange and the tired wife
Dried by the recurring sun of her kitchen.
Now it is electric eleven o'clock – the stewing meat
Smells savoury past the pruned back roses
And wafts on the street's spindly limits,
The only fragrance of defence and love.

Metamorphosis

This new Daks suit, greeny-brown,
Oyster coloured buttons, single vent, tapered
Trousers, no waistcoat, hairy tweed – my own:
A suit to show responsibility, to show
Return to life – easily got for two pounds down
Paid off in six months – the first stage in the change.
I am only the image I can force upon the town.

The town will have me: I stalk in glass,
A thin reflection in the windows, best
In jewellers' velvet backgrounds – I don't pass,
I stop, elect to look at wedding rings –
My figure filled with clothes, my putty mask,
A face fragrant with arrogance, stuffed
With recognition – I am myself at last.

I wait in the pub with my Worthington.
Then you come in – how many days did love have,
How can they be catalogued again?
We talk of how we miss each other – I tell
Some truth – you, cruel stories built of men:
'It wasn't good at first but he's improving.'
More talk about his car, his drinks, his friends.

I look to the wild mirror at the bar –
A beautiful girl smiles beside me – she's real
And her regret is real. If only I had a car,
If only – my stately self cringes, renders down;
As in a werewolf film I'm horrible, far
Below the collar – my fingers crack, my tyrant suit
Chokes me as it hugs me in its fire.

Death's Morning Shadows

It's light, here's thumping in the pipes – spit
Sounds in the wall, a tap's settled sob.
Water in my eyes – I have some sleep left – in it
I can watch my Father. They'll have a job
To kill him but they're going to – a minute
From now he'll be dragged off by the mob.

Caught by a bellied tear I come awake.
Espresso sugar pricks an eyeball.
I press sleep back into my eyes – a lake
Of grinning water holds no splash – slow crawl
(I'm a stylish sleep swimmer), then the ache
Of overarm, the sound of waterfall.

I'll gear the dream to sex. That sharp face
Is with me now – it will not let me use
Its landlocked body. I try to kiss a place
Where I have been. It scolds, its words refuse
My tongueing. I am naked, in disgrace
With love, skulking under its high-heeled shoes.

Quick change to the toothache dream. I'm in pain
But know I am only a man and tooth in bed.
The pain in me hunts my flesh – my name
Locked in the alarm clock bursts my head.
The lit room rings with morning and again
I hear the sore pipes singing for the dead.

Beast and the Beauty

His fear never loud in daylight, risen to a night whisper
Of a dead mother in the weatherboard house,
He had this great piece of luck: a girl
In Paris clothes, ex-school monitor, chose
Him for her lover. Twenty-one and experienced,
She showed his hands the presentiment of clothes
And first at a party kissed him, then took
Him home where they did what he'd always supposed.

Her sophistication was his great delight:
Her mother and father drinking, throwing things,
The unhappy marriage, the tradespeople on Christian
Name terms – all the democratic sexiness – mornings
With the Pick of the Pops and the *Daily Express*
And yet the sudden itching despair, the wonder in King's
College Chapel, the depth that lived in her soul
Of which this raciness was only the wordly covering.

But the sophistication chose to kill – the itch
Was on the inside of the skin. Her family of drunks
Were shrewd, wine-wise young barristers and gentlemen-
Farmers fought for her hand. In the loft there waited
    trunks
Of heirlooms to be taken seriously. He found himself
Ditched, his calls unanswered, his world shrunk
To eating in Lyons', waiting outside her house at
    midnight,
Her serious tears to haunt him, boiling on his bunk.

So he sits alone in Libraries, hideous and hairy of soul,
A beast again, waiting for a lustful kiss to bring
Back his human smell, the taste of woman on his tongue.

Lament for a Proprietor

This was the end of a man but also died
Ten suits, twenty shirts, Clare College ties
And scarves, a Radiogram, one hundred dance discs
And Vivaldi's *Seasons*, shells picked up
On Sark and Ibiza, Phaidon and Skira books
Coverless and crooked – twenty invitations
To Balls and Bottle Parties, some still to be held,
Gin, Whisky, Cointreau, Kirsch, Drambuie,
And an unopened letter from his mother,
An unfinished letter to a Rowing Coach,
As his Granny was still alive the pots of cash
He would inherit did not die, but who
Could breathe life back into his possessions,
Put Humpty Dumpty safe on the high sea wall?
They died for him since he had lived for them.
In death they share a room – nobody knows
He was alive now all his things are dead.

What a Lying Lot the Writers Are

To put it all down now I take my pencil up
And a bilge of hate can be sluiced up top.
I have no time in a bored lifetime
To love a body in its sour confines
Because the love is a meeting place
Of impossible pictures on a disputed face.

But people make metaphysics out of this
And play among bodies with a such or thus.
Their eyes picture a world but they call
What they cannot see, Heaven or Hell.
To be above the tearing fingers of the ruck
You need good teeth, a good income, good luck.

This then is the lie: we write and perform
Great solemnities in the mind's frame.
The lovely are loved, the victims rail,
Beds hold the sick and the hale free-wheel,
Great events are remembered as history,
Science understands us, we are free.

Books tell us stories of friendship and love,
Animals and plants help us stay alive.
Talking until the last minimum of death
We praise God or opportunity or both
But we die in the first room we see,
The bright locked world, the captivity.

John Marston Advises Anger

All the boys are howling to take the girls to bed.
Our betters say it's a seedy world. The critics say
Think of them as an Elizabethan Chelsea set.
Then they've never listened to our lot — no talk
Could be less like – but the bodies are the same:
Those jeans and bums and sweaters of the King's
    Road
Would fit Marston's stage. What's in a name,
If Cheapside and the Marshalsea mean Eng. Lit.
And the Fantasie, Sa Tortuga, Grisbi, Bongi-Bo
Mean life? A cliché? What hurts dies on paper,
Fades to classic pain. Love goes as the M.G. goes.
The colonel's daughter in black stockings, hair
Like sash cords, face iced white, studies art,
Goes home once a month. She won't marry the men
She sleeps with, she'll revert to type — it's part
Of the side-show: Mummy and Daddy in the wings,
The bongos fading on the road to Haslemere
Where the inheritors are inheriting still,
Marston's Malheureux found his whore too dear;
Today some Jazz Club girl on the social make
Would put him through his paces, the aphrodisiac
    cruel.
His friends would be the smoothies of our Elizabethan
    age –
The Rally Men, Grantchester Breakfast Men, Public
    School
Personal Assistants and the fragrant P.R.O.s,
Cavalry-twilled tame publishers praising Logue,
Classics Honours Men promoting Jazzetry,
Market Researchers married into Vogue.
It's a Condé Nast world and so Marston's was.

His had a real gibbet – our death's out of sight.
The same thin richness of these worlds remains –
The flesh-packed jeans, the car-stung appetite
Volley on his stage, the cage of discontent.

Made in Heaven

From Heals and Harrods come her lovely bridegrooms
(One cheque alone furnished two bedrooms),

From a pantechnicon in the dog-paraded street
Under the orange plane leaves, on workmen's feet

Crunching over Autumn, the fruits of marriage brought
Craftsman-felt wood, Swedish dressers, a court

Stool tastefully imitated and the wide bed –
(the girl who married money kept her maiden head).

As things were ticked off the Harrods list, there grew
A middle-class maze to pick your way through –

The labour-saving kitchen to match the labour-saving
thing
She'd fitted before marriage (O Love, with this ring

I thee wed) – lastly the stereophonic radiogram
And her Aunt's sly letter promising a pram.

Settled in now, the Italian honeymoon over,
As the relatives said, she was living in clover.

The discontented drinking of a few weeks stopped,
She woke up one morning to her husband's alarm-clock,

Saw the shining faces of the wedding gifts from the bed,
Foresaw the cosy routine of the massive years ahead.

As she watched her husband knot his tie for the city,
She thought: I wanted to be a dancer once – it's a pity

I've done none of the things I thought I wanted to,
Found nothing more exacting than my own looks, got
    through

Half a dozen lovers whose faces I can't quite remember
(I can still start the Rose Adagio, one foot on the fender)

But at least I'm safe from everything but cancer –
The apotheosis of the young wife and mediocre dancer.

South of the Duodenum

Not everybody wants to live. When they carted away
Old Terrestrial to hospital, he had been
Eighty years an inmate of his smoky house
And he went up blue to Heaven asking why.
The answer was endemic to the voice.
Eighty years dead, at last death quits the brain.

Keeping alive in jealous pools of eyes, astir
At windowings of Vogue or such
A conniving click of a car door, this innocence
Is life's. Come up like the moon upon the stars
The great wash of death makes no pretence;
A perfect scansion drops at this approach.

O the cancer atolls, growing by writing light
In money's time – you are the machines
Of hate and love. Here nothing trusts itself
But in your proof: early to live, the late
Body blooms in your garrulous health –
At your deathbed both killer and victim shine.

Death in the Pergola Tea-Rooms

Snakes are hissing behind the misted glass.
Inside there are tea urns of rubicund copper, chromium
    pipes
Pissing steam, a hot rattle of cups, British
Institutional Thickness. Under a covering of yellowing
    glass
Or old celluloid, cress-and-tomato, tongue-and-ham
Sandwiches shine complacently, skewered
By 1/6 a round. The wind spitefully lays the door shut
On a slow customer – ten pairs of eyes track
To his fairisle jersey; for a few seconds voices drop
Lower than the skirmishing of steam.
Outside by the river bank, the local doctor
Gets out of his '47 Vauxhall, sucking today's
Twentieth cigarette. He stops and throws it
Down in the mud of the howling orchard.
The orchard's crouching, half-back trees take the wind
On a pass from the poplars of the other bank,
Under the scooping wind, a conveyor-belt of wrinkles,
The buckled river cuts the cramping fields.

Just out of rattle reach and sound of cup clang,
The old rationalist is dying in the Pergola.
Two Labour Party friends and the doctor
Rearrange his woven rugs. The blood is roaring
In his head, the carcinoma commune, the fronde
Of pain rule in his brain – the barricades have broken
In his bowels – it is the rule of spasm, the terror sits.
He knows he is dying, he has a business of wills,
Must make a scaffolding for his wife with words,
Fit the flames in his head into the agenda.
Making up his mind now, he knows it is right

To take the body through committee meetings and
    campaign rooms
To wear it and patch it like a good tweed; to come to
The fraying ends of its time, have to get the doctor
To staple up its seams just to keep the fingers
Pulling blankets up, stroking comfort on other fingers,
Patting the warm patch where the cat has been.
There is no God. It is winter, the windows sing
And stealthy sippers linger with their tea.
Now rushing a bare branch, the wind tips up
The baleful embroidery of cold drops
On a spider's web. Inside the old man's body
The draught is from an open furnace door – outside the
    room,
Ignoring the doctor's mild professional face,
The carnival winter like the careful God
Lays on sap-cold rosetrees and sour flower beds
The cruel confusion of its disregard.

Party Line

The bottles redly close an unborn sound.
Here come the liberators who will set
Free actions which were tightly bound.
Aggressors in jeans and evening dress, the brash
Music of these fitted marmosets,
Brimming in clothes, brings the bated crash:
This is splendid value for a pound.

One girl undressed because she thought it right;
Another, trained in truth, watched what she did
Loving her mirrored love, her second sight.
A judge of conduct gasped to see the fun,
A valued impotence safe in his head –
A private creature staring out the sun
Not warmed by it is seeing by its light.

O this is arrogant the dancers say.
The conjured revellers are just in touch,
Which witness moves them dancing as they sway.
Wallflowers at School Balls and pimply men,
Wanting love and made to want too much,
May not be saved; ceremonious haters then,
Their world rebels where first it would obey.

All coats lie fallen on the party floor
Where an angry guest threw them one by one.
The permutations of love are finished for
One evening. Here we go home, out
Of reach of drunken communion,
Secular saints who do without
Power, a pleasure left behind the door.

But to these aspirations everything belongs.
Here is the bed's silence, the parcel of
A dream wrapped in dirty songs
Pillow-rehearsed: it is five o'clock
When nobody is making love –
The body floats in the mind, a shock
Of sleep comes, steeped in party wrongs.

The Historians Call Up Pain

When his father died still apostate,
The new Emperor took his grandfather's name
(The eighth to be so called) and appointed
The most zealous Inquisitor
History has yet recorded. In the subject lands,
The Eastern Pale, the prosperous Low Countries,
And even in his own great hinterland,
Ten thousand heretics were burnt to death
In one year. Men dreamed of Millennium
The more; martyrs died soundlessly at the stake,
Their eyes hotter than the flames. The Emperor
Caused his father's grave to be opened
And sent the Pope his bones packed in the ashes
Of a thousand Adamites. This, of course, was
Six centuries ago: today this persecution
Is a best bet Honours question
In the History Tripos; it has also provided
Several specious parallels for Marxists
Praising Thomas Muntzer and American Scholars
Screening for chiliasm. Yet if we keep
Our minds on the four last things
And join the historians on their frieze of pain
We may forget our world of milk gone stale,
Cancer touches in the afternoon, girls in Jensens,
Gramophone records scratched and warped,
Managers fattening tumours of ambition.
We cannot know what John of Leyden felt
Under the Bishop's tongs – we can only
Walk in temperate London, our educated city,
Wishing to cry as freely as they did who died
In the Age of Faith. We have our loneliness
And our regret with which to build an eschatology.

Annotations of Auschwitz

I

When the burnt flesh is finally at rest,
The fires in the asylum grates will come up
And wicks turn down to darkness in the madman's eyes.

II

My suit is hairy, my carpet smells of death,
My toothbrush handle grows a cuticle.
I have six million foulnesses of breath.
Am I mad? The doctor holds my testicles
While the room fills with the zyklon B I cough.

III

On Piccadilly underground I fall asleep –
I shuffle with the naked to the steel door,
Now I am only ten from the front – I wake up –
We are past Gloucester Rd, I am not a Jew,
But scratches web the ceiling of the train.

IV

Around staring buildings the pale flowers grow;
The frenetic butterfly, the bee made free by work,
Rouse and rape the pollen pads, the nectar stoops.
The rusting railway ends here. The blind end in Europe's
gut.
Touch one piece of unstrung barbed wire –
Let it taste blood: let one man scream in pain,
Death's Botanical Gardens can flower again.

V

A man eating his dressing in the hospital
Is lied to by his stomach. It's a final feast to him
Of beef, blood pudding and black bread.
The orderly can't bear to see this mimic face
With its prim accusing picture after death.
On the stiff square a thousand bodies
Dig up useless ground – he hates them all,
These lives ignoble as ungoverned glands.
They fatten in statistics everywhere
And with their sick, unkillable fear of death
They crowd out peace from executioners' sleep.

VI

Forty thousand bald men drowning in a stream –
The like of light on all those bobbing skulls
Has never been seen before. Such death, says the painter,
Is worthwhile – it makes a colour never known.
It makes a sight that's unimagined, says the poet.
It's nothing to do with me, says the man who hates
The poet and the painter. Six million deaths can hardly
Occur at once. What do they make? Perhaps
An idiot's normalcy. I need never feel afraid
When I salt the puny snail – cruelty's grown up
And waits for time and men to bring into its hands
The snail's adagio and all the taunting life
Which has not cared about or guessed its tortured
    scope.

VII

London is full of chickens on electric spits,
    Cooking in windows where the public pass.
This, say the chickens, is their Auschwitz,
    And all poultry eaters are psychopaths.

Who Gets the Pope's Nose

It is so tiring having to look after the works of God.
　　The sea will run away
　　From martyrs' feet, gay
Dissipated Florentines kiss tumours out of a man's head,
Scheduled liquefactions renew saints' blood,

In Andean villages starved Inca girls
　　Develop the stigmata,
　　Dying dogs pronounce the Pater
Noster on the vivisection table, the World
Press report trachoma'd eyes that drip wide pearls.

All investigated, all authenticated, all
　　Miracles beyond doubt.
　　Yet messengers go in and out,
The Vatican fills up with paper. The faithful
Work for a Merchant God who deals in souls.

Was there ever a man in Nazareth who was King of
　　　　Kings?
　　There is a fat man in Rome
　　To guide his people home.
Bring back the rack and set the bones straining,
For faith needs pain to help with its explaining.

Fill a glass with water and gaze into it.
　　There is the perfect rule
　　Which no God can repeal.
Having to cope with death, the extraordinary visit,
Ordinary man swills in a holy sweat.

And high above Rome in a room with wireless
　　The Pope also waits to die.
　　God is the heat in July
And the iron band of pus tightening in the chest.
Of all God's miracles, death is the greatest.

Too Worn to Wear

Dear Lie, between the trusting chair
And bashful fire, a world enough
(Though schizophrenic air
   Divides its real to worn and rare)
Purports to watch; the red cough
Pastilles know the need they share
With mucous, a rage of stuff
Wasted upon a shift of air.

Old fashioned issue done in pleats –
Desire compels again to shock
(Barbarous islands in the heat
   Bake fetishes but don't grow wheat);
This image is made by decanter and lock –
Such a spine for poison's seat
Her continuum is, oceans knock
The dead fish at her wading feet.

By severed cages outer eyes
Choose bars to hang; in pots
(Once in an Age of Black Surmise
   Virgins bled but had no sighs)
A way of life paid in through slots
Just grows to grow, not otherwise.
So trespass passes, here who rots
Comes strangely back to health crabwise.

Mild danger and yet in mild
Contempt love is quite lost.
(The model railway plays the child
   Home out of the felt and wild)
But now unable to bear the cost

Carnival whim, the depthless smile
Vamps on private Pentecost
The history of a green exile.

•

Phar Lap in the Melbourne Museum

A masterpiece of the taxidermist's art,
Australia's top patrician stares
Gravely ahead at crowded emptiness.
As if alive, the lustre of dead hairs,
Lozenged liquid eyes, black nostrils
Gently flared, otter-satin coat declares
That death cannot visit in this thin perfection.

The democratic hero full of guile,
Noble, handsome, gentle Houyhnhnm
(In both Paddock and St Leger difference is
    Lost in the welter of money) – to see him win
Men sold farms, rode miles in floods,
Stole money, locked up wives, somehow got in:
First away, he led the field and easily won.

It was his simple excellence to be best.
Tough men owned him, their minds beset
By stakes, bookies' doubles, crooked jocks.
He soon became a byword, public asset,
A horse with a nation's soul upon his back –
Australia's Ark of the Covenent, set
Before the people, perfect, loved like God.

And like God to be betrayed by friends.
Sent to America, he died of poisoned food.
In Australia children cried to hear the news
(This Prince of Orange knew no bad or good).
It was, as people knew, a plot of life:
To live in strength, to excel and die too soon,
So they drained his body and they stuffed his skin.

Twenty years later on Sunday afternoons
You still can't see him for the rubbing crowds.
He shares with Bradman and Ned Kelly some
Of the dirty jokes you still can't say out loud.
It is Australian innocence to love
The naturally excessive and be proud
Of a thoroughbred bay gelding who ran fast.

Your Attention Please

The Polar DEW has just warned that
A nuclear rocket strike of
At least one thousand megatons
Has been launched by the enemy
Directly at our major cities.
This announcement will take
Two and a quarter minutes to make,
You therefore have a further
Eight and a quarter minutes
To comply with the shelter
Requirements published in the Civil
Defence Code – section Atomic Attack.
A specially shortened Mass
Will be broadcast at the end
Of this announcement –
Protestant and Jewish services
Will begin simultaneously –
Select your wavelength immediately
According to instructions
In the Defence Code. Do not
Take well-loved pets (including birds)
Into your shelter – they will consume
Fresh air. Leave the old and bed-
ridden, you can do nothing for them.
Remember to press the sealing
Switch when everyone is in
The shelter. Set the radiation
Aerial, turn on the geiger barometer.
Turn off your Television now.
Turn off your radio immediately
The Services end. At the same time
Secure explosion plugs in the ears

Of each member of your family. Take
Down your plasma flasks. Give your children
The pills marked one and two
In the C.D. green container, then put
Them to bed. Do not break
The inside airlock seals until
The radiation All Clear shows
(Watch for the cuckoo in your
perspex panel), or your District
Touring Doctor rings your bell.
If before this, your air becomes
Exhausted or if any of your family
Is critically injured, administer
The capsules marked 'Valley Forge'
(Red pocket in No. 1 Survival Kit)
For painless death. (Catholics
Will have been instructed by their priests
What to do in this eventuality.)
This announcement is ending. Our President
Has already given orders for
Massive retaliation – it will be
Decisive. Some of us may die.
Remember, statistically
It is not likely to be you.
All flags are flying fully dressed
On Government buildings – the sun is shining.
Death is the least we have to fear.
We are all in the hands of God,
Whatever happens happens by His Will.
Now go quickly to your shelters.

Reading a Novel

Where did the headache come from? On page 10
The hero's at his Prep School – he can't tie
His tie, the Matron scolds him – and then
Page 90, he's humiliated by a girl
He tries to seduce at the University.
The reader's forehead fronts the painful world.

These simulacrums act. Page 136 –
National Serviceman crying in a hut;
The hero fails to help; our guilt now sticks.
Put the novel down, it wasn't like that,
Each case is different; the headache taps, but
Still read on – discontent seeks facts.

People we've met before – that party scene
Where all the girls were out of Salad Days;
The hero's self-examination's been
Primed by disgust: 'Why do I want to know
Such people.' The want is simple and it stays.
Self-satisfaction puts on the best show.

It had to come – the hero's on the Downs
Surrounded by roses in a Mental Home.
Visitors look at basket work, the sounds
Of an electric mower patrol the ward.
We've reached page 201, he's not alone;
The girl on the sun terrace keeps the interest stirred.

'A saga of self-satisfied embarrassment.'
Quotation from the *Observer*'s tough review.
Are we ashamed we liked it? It went
Well with last week's gloom. Things were much
Easier at the end when the hero found his true
Role – the man who looks and sees and is not
      touched.

Healthy with headaches, this is modern life.
Overworked reviewers long for the heroic
But novelists who give a man-and-wife
Commentary about the eavesdropped bed,
Garish with certainty, trite with tact, still stick
To their proper work: the clichéd mask, the daily
    bread.

Two Polemical Sonnets

I
1920–1960

Then the grass grew over men's marrowless bones,
Twelve million dead and Europe at peace again.
Birkenhead's sword to hand, ambitious men
Dined at heavy tables antlered with lights – phones
Rang Press Lords' midnight injunctions – the pen
Mightier than the sword carved the world into zones;
The old order was not dead, it raised new loans
From democracy – names became numinous with a
    hyphen.

Now the glittering prizes have pimple-free skin:
Welfare milk and orange improve the standard of
    mistress's looks,
Each sexy Susan is some nobleman's kin.
Conscious of clothes, you take God seriously,
Are interested in the world and review travel books;
Your winey tongue has tamed the whisky spirit of F.E.

II
A HIGH-BORN LADY CONDENSES HER MEMOIRS
FOR *READER'S DIGEST*

The long littleness has been so long.
My generation inherited responsibility
Along with its looks. If they'd lived, the golden boys
    would be
As old now as Henry James was, that swan-song
Afternoon on the Cam – as old now as me.
The bullets were kept for the young – the Somme
Brought together those who could never belong
Together, the two faces of England, bled to equality.

The widows of Swindon lost their husbands' pay,
But we were cheated of our birthright, a neatly feudal
World equipped with modern excitements. So the only
    way
Was to lead the fashions – drinks, parties, the stage.
We've kept our place even if we haven't kept very well –
Time and geography robbed us of a heritage.

Legend

We walk home past
   Silver and salted fish
As the first rain strikes
   The five-storied town
To be marooned with tea
   In a room and waspish
Waiting for music
   Walk up and down.

And when it comes
   The tea tray shakes,
The pinned-up prints
   With curled edges fold;
Sitting on the bed
   And holding hands makes
The green rain in the trees
   Violent and cold.

Keep me close dear,
   We listen by heart
To caravans of music
   From Sheba and Ophir.
Comforted by pain
   In the red desert, they start
With jewels of murder
   For each quarter of the year.

From Ophir with gold
   And indulgent spice
Into green lands of light
   Yellow sands blowing
One way, it brings tribute

To our precious avarice
Of touching; it unskeins
The skin of journeying.

Somme and Flanders

Who am I to speak up for the long dead?
Three uncles I never knew say I'm right.
Their tongues are speaking in my head
I'm related to their flesh by fright.

Their world was made of nerves and mud.
Reading about it now shocks me – Haig
Gets transfusions of their blood,
Plum-and-apple feeds them for the plague.

Those Harmsworth books have sepia'd
Their peasants' fields sown with barbed-wire.
In Nineteen-Nineteen, crops of crosses appeared
Seeded by bodies ripened in shell-fire.

One image haunts us who have read of death
In Auschwitz in our time – it is just light,
Shivering men breathing rum crouch beneath
The sandbag parapet – left to right

The line goes up and over the top,
Serious in gas masks, bayonets fixed,
Slowly forward – the swearing shells have stopped –
Somewhere ahead of them death's stopwatch ticks.

Soliloquy at Potsdam

There are always the poor –
Getting themselves born in crowded houses,
Feeding on the parish, losing their teeth early
And learning to dodge blows, getting
Strong bodies – cases for the warped nut of the mind.
The masterful cat o' nine tails, the merciful
Discipline of the hours of drill – better
Than being poor in crowded Europe, the swan-
    swept
Waters where the faces dredge for bread
And the soggy dead are robbed on their way to the
    grave.
I can hear it from this window, the musket-drill
On the barrack square. Later today I'll visit
The punishment block. Who else in Europe
Could take these verminous, clutching creatures
And break them into men? What of the shredded
    back
And the broken pelvis, when the side-drum sounds,
When the uniformed wave tilts and overwhelms
The cheese-trading burghers' world, the aldermanic
Principalities. The reformers sit at my table,
They talk well but they've never seen a battle
Or watched the formed brain in the flogged body
Marching to death on a bellyful of soup and orders.
There has to be misery so there can be discipline.
People will have to die because I cannot bear
Their clinging to life. Why are the best trumpeters
Always French? Watch the west, the watershed
Of revolution. Now back to Quantz. I like to think
That in an afternoon of three sonatas
A hundred regiments have marched more miles

Than lie between here and Vienna and not once
Has a man broken step. Who would be loved
If he could be feared and hated, yet still
Enjoy his lust, eat well and play the flute?

Nine O'Clock Thoughts on the 73 Bus

Client meeting at twelve, that lot of layabouts
Will have to be spoken up for, must tell Ann
To get a new ivy for the office, louts
I saw trying to touch her up, lovely bum
Though. Everyone tries to get as much sex as he can,
The copywriter is flushed by the client's sun.

Ghosts

I

A large woman in a kimono, her flesh
Already sweating in the poulticing heat
Of afternoon – just from her bath, she stands,
Propping her foot on a chair of faded pink,
Preparing to cut her corns. The sun
Simmers through the pimply glass – as if
Inside a light bulb, the room is lit with heat.
The window is the sun's lens, its dusty slice
Of light falls on the woman's foot. The woman
Is my Mother – the clicking of her scissors
Fascinates the little feminine boy
In striped shirt, Tootal tie, thick woollen socks,
His garters down. Memory insists the boy is me.
The house still stands where we stood then.
The inheritance I had, her only child,
Was her party melancholy and a body
Thickening like hers, the wide-pored flesh
Death broke into twenty years ago.

II

The red wind carrying dust on to my Sunday shoes
Reddens also my nostrils and my mouth.
I stand by the school's venerable, fifty-years-old,
Washed cement veranda, waiting for my Father.
The Bunya pines along the straggling drive
Drop chunky cones on gravel – windswept bees
Slog across the Masters' Garden to lemon flowers;
Boys shout, dogs bark, no second is quite silent.
My Father with the Headmaster comes to me.
It is Sunday, Parents' Visiting Day. The drive
Is churned by cars. When we go down town,
Despite milk shakes and a demure high tea
In the Canberra Temperance Hotel, I only sulk.
I have kept this priggishness, Father;
The smart world laps you round. Your fear of this
Small child is now my fear – my boarding-school
World of rules rules me – my ghost
Has caught me up to sit and judge
The nightmares that I have, memories of love.

III

My Mother married all that there was left
Of an Old Colonial Family. The money gone,
The family house remained, surrounded by the dogs
He'd buried, forty years a bachelor –
We came there every Sunday in a silver tram
For tennis, when my Mother was alive.
Sometimes I try to find my face in theirs:
My Father in the Lacrosse team, my Mother
Nursing in the War – they tell no story
In family photographs. Their city is changed;
Coca-cola bottles bounce upon their lawn,
No one grows flowers, picnics are no fun,
Their aviaries are full of shop-bought birds.
Who goes for week-ends down the Bay
In thirty footers to St Helena, Peel and Jumpin' Pin?
No yachts stand off the Old People's Home,
Out past the crab-pot buoys and floating mangrove fruit.

I was born late in a late marriage. Psychiatrists
Say it makes no difference – but now I think
Of what was never said in a tropical house
Of five miscarriages. If the words were said
They'd start the deaths up that I left for dead.

A Mass for Money

The soft hands with fat rings move on
The white tablecloth – the rich are dining out.
The grey nosing people are away,
Who lift these bodies where they belong.
Waiters only mutter in the kitchen and never shout:
They are in service to noise and must obey.

My aunt and uncle are rich and now quite old.
They never gave a party for lust or fun
But, wonderful hosts, they would entertain
Buyers, Directors, difficult wives – a cold
Sincerity sits in their faces now – they've retired in the
    sun
By the seaside. All they want is to avoid pain,

But it is my envy sets their pace of wealth.
It chromes the plain work of an appetite.
I can imagine a Second Empire Love Nest
In a simple arrangement for suburban health.
Such riches deck the rich despite
The plain flesh on view, paid-for, well-processed.

Death makes no difference. No such full stop
Threatens the full mouth or the speeding car.
Fortune and misfortune stretch infinite.
I think of love and inequality. At the top,
I say, there are words which feeling cannot mar
But here there is only money and the use of it.

Index of First Lines

THE PENGUIN MODERN POETS

*NOT FOR SALE IN THE U.S.A.
†NOT FOR SALE IN THE U.S.A. OR CANADA